Days 7 to

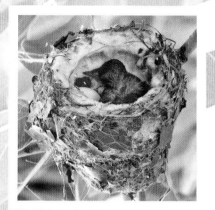

Day 7

Day 8

Day 9

Day 10

Day 11

Day 12

To Calvin,
Happy birding!
Susanne Strauss

Sunnystyle Books

www.sunnystylebooks.com

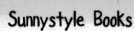

Susanne Strauss

Author & Photographer

714-600-0683

sunnystylebooks@att.net

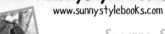

sunnystylebooks   ▶ Susanne Strauss

Little Jewel's Remarkable Journey

Story and photography by Susanne Strauss

Published by Sunnystyle Books
PO Box 715
Placentia, CA 92871

www.sunnystylebooks

10 9 8 7 6 5 4 3 2 1

ISBN: 978-1-7342267-0-6

Library of Congress Control Number: 2019920248

Printed in the United States of America

This book is dedicated to all those who admire and are fascinated by hummingbirds.

Enjoy!

Little Jewel is inside the tiny egg in the nest.
The egg is smaller than a penny.

Momma Jewel sits on the egg all day and night to keep the egg warm. She will incubate the egg for about 20 days.

The nest is hidden in the tree so that predators

like hawks

and scrub-jays

cannot find Little Jewel!

Little Jewel hatched out of the egg a few days ago.
She has no feathers to keep herself warm.

Momma Jewel quietly flies onto the nest. She will keep Little Jewel warm and safe.

Little Jewel's beak is bright orange. Momma Jewel can easily find her beak to feed her.

Momma Jewel feeds Little Jewel nectar and insects
by regurgitating, or throwing up, into her mouth.
Yum! Yum!

Little Jewel is blind for the first several days. So, although you can see her, she cannot see you.

Momma Jewel often visits Little Jewel. She stays on the nest and watches Little Jewel after feeding her.

Day 7

Day 8

As she grows,
Little Jewel
sleeps …

and sleeps …

Day 9

and sleeps.

Little Jewel now has many pin feathers. Her colored feathers are also starting to show.

Little Jewel's wings are growing longer. Soon she will use her wings to fly forwards, backwards, and sideways!

Momma Jewel has stayed on the nest every night.
Tonight is her last night on the nest.

Little Jewel's beak is growing longer and changing colors.

Little Jewel still sleeps most of the day.

Momma Jewel
is always
close by.
She protects
Little Jewel to
keep her safe.

Little Jewel can finally see you! There is so much
to look at - the leaves, the ladybugs,
and her mom.

Momma Jewel is so beautiful. See her gorget, the feathers around her throat? These feathers are shiny in the sunshine.

Little Jewel now has tiny tail feathers. She can also stretch across the whole nest!

Little Jewel often goes to the bathroom.
She carefully aims outside of the nest.

Little
Jewel
keeps
growing

Day
19

Day
20

and
growing.

The nest seems to be getting smaller
or is Little Jewel getting bigger?

Little Jewel sits on top of the nest
and looks at the world.

Little Jewel
starts
stretching.

She
carefully
stretches
one wing at
a time.

Little Jewel enjoys fluffing herself.
It feels so good. Try it!

Little Jewel's beautiful mom
is fluffing herself too.

Little Jewel hears her mom flying nearby. Momma Jewel will be feeding her soon. Yay!

Momma Jewel is back! She still feeds Little Jewel many times a day. Little Jewel loves her mom.

Little Jewel has a super long tongue. She will use it to lap nectar. Right now that leaf looks tasty.

Little Jewel loves flapping because it makes her wings stronger.

Whew! Now it is time to rest.

Little Jewel is almost fully grown and has all her coloring.
She is very beautiful just like her mom.

This is
Little Jewel's
last day
in the nest.

Little Jewel
enjoys
preening,
or cleaning,
her feathers.

Oh, look!
Little Jewel
found some
bugs to eat.
Yum! Yum!

Little Jewel loves when her mom visits her. Momma Jewel takes great care of Little Jewel.

Little Jewel is perfecting her flapping because she is almost ready to fly off.

She takes one last look around.

Off she goes ...
Wish her luck!

Little Jewel just flew to her first branch. She is now ready to explore the world. Where will she go next?

About the Hummingbirds

Little Jewel and
Momma Jewel are
Allen's Hummingbirds.

Allen's Hummingbirds
nest mostly in California
and southern Oregon.

Allen's Hummingbird Female

The female builds the nest
and takes care of the young.

The female has shiny green feathers
on her backside, cinnamon-orange
feathers on her sides, white feathers
on her chest, and tiny bronze spots
and a bigger central spot of shiny
orange-red feathers on her throat.

The male also has shiny green feathers
on his backside, but he has more cinnamon-orange
feathers than the female and shiny orange-red feathers
on his throat.

Allen's Hummingbird Male

Attracting Hummingbirds to Your Garden

Tips to Attract Hummingbirds

In your garden, add

- colorful tubular flowers,
- hummingbird feeders with sugar water, and
- a water fountain or bird bath with a mister.

Sugar Water Recipe

Ingredients

- Sugar (1 part)
- Water (4 parts)

Directions

1. Boil water.
2. As soon as water boils, add sugar.
3. Stir until sugar is dissolved. (Do not add red food coloring.)
4. Let cool.
5. Pour into feeder.
6. Watch for hungry hummingbirds!

Fun Story Facts

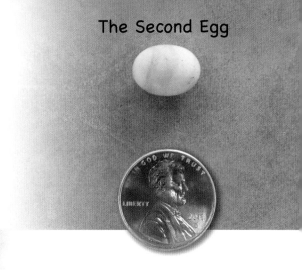

The Second Egg

The Eggs

Momma Jewel laid two eggs; however only one egg hatched. The second egg stayed in the nest with Little Jewel while she grew up.

The Nest

Momma Jewel decorated the nest with chips of blue paint that had peeled from the wrought iron fence. She made the coolest nest in the neighborhood!

Blue Paint Chips

Back Cover Photograph

On Day 27, Little Jewel flew out of the garden and into the field to sip nectar from a pink tubular-shaped flower.

About the Author

Susanne Strauss is a writer, award-winning photographer, and nature enthusiast.

One year, a mother hummingbird built a nest in her garden and laid two eggs. After the first egg hatched, Susanne took pictures each day to document the growth of the baby hummingbird and the interactions between the baby and mother. The photographs inspired the story of Little Jewel.

Susanne lives in Southern California. After Little Jewel's remarkable journey, many more Allen's Hummingbirds have visited her garden and raised their young in the same tree in which Momma Jewel raised Little Jewel.

For Little Jewel hummingbird-themed activities, visit sunnystylebooks.com

Little Jewel's Day-by-Day Growth
Days 13 to 18

Day 13

Day 14

Day 15

Day 16

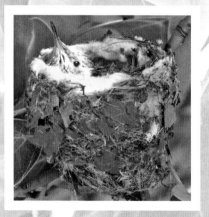

Day 17

Day 18